A Song of Elsewhere

First published in 2015 by
The Dedalus Press
13 Moyclare Road
Baldoyle
Dublin 13
Ireland

www.dedaluspress.com

Copyright © Gerard Smyth, 2015

ISBN 978 1 910251 07 2

All rights reserved.
No part of this publication may be reproduced in any form or by
any means without the prior permission of the publisher.

The moral right of the author has been asserted.

Dedalus Press titles are represented in the UK by
Central Books, 99 Wallis Road, London E9 5LN
and in North America by Syracuse University Press, Inc.,
621 Skytop Road, Suite 110, Syracuse, New York 13244.

Cover image: 'Return Journey' by Martin Gale,
by kind permission of the artist

The Dedalus Press receives financial assistance from
The Arts Council / An Chomhairle Ealaíon

A Song of Elsewhere

Gerard Smyth

DEDALUS PRESS
DUBLIN, IRELAND

ACKNOWLEDGEMENTS

Acknowledgements are due to the editors of the following publications where some of these poems, or versions of them, first appeared: *Abridged*, *Agenda*, *Bare Hands anthology*, *The Clifden Anthology*, *Cork Literary Review*, *Cyphers*, *Fusion* (Boston), *Irish Pages*, *The Moth*, *Poetry Ireland Review*, *Poetry Review*, *Prairie Schooner* (Nebraska), *The SHop*, *The Irish Times*, *The Warwick Review*, *Stone Water Review* (St Paul, Minnesota), *The Stony Thursday Book*, *Windows*, and the online journals *The Burning Bush Two*, *Fusion*, *The Honest Ulsterman*, *North West Words*, *Manchester Review* and *Southword Online*.

Also in the anthologies: *A Second Meath Anthology* (ed. Tom French); *Berryman's Fate: A Centenary Celebration in Verse* (ed. Philip Coleman); *Dogs Singing* (ed. Jessie Lendennie), *This Landscape's Fierce Embrace: The Poetry of Francis Harvey* (ed. Donna L Potts); *What We Found There; Poets Respond to the Treasures of the National Museum of Ireland* (ed. Theo Dorgan). A number of poems were first published in translation: in German on *lyrikline* and in *Park 66* (Berlin, translation by Richard Pietrass); *La Traductiere* (Paris, translation by Maryline Bertoncini); *Journal de Poetes* (Brussels, translation by Cecile Dubois) and *Irodalmi Jelen* (Budapest, translation by Thomas Kabdebo).

Thanks too to Irish Literature Exchange for its support of the translations.

'When All the Birds Were Called Away' was printed in a limited broadside edition at Traffic Street Press, St Paul, Minnesota and 'Islandbridge' appeared as a limited edition broadside from The Distillers Press, National College of Art and Design, Dublin. 'The Things We Keep' and 'The Blackbirds of Wilkinstown' were written as part of a collaboration with the artist Angela O'Kelly for *Out of the Marvellous,* an exhibition in the National Craft Centre in Kilkenny and Solstice Arts Centre in Navan.

Several of the poems were broadcast on RTÉ Radio One, on *Sunday Miscellany, South Wind Blows* and *Arts Tonight.*

The author is also grateful to the Centre Culturel Irlandais, Paris, for a residency in May/June 2013, during which several of these poems were written.

Contents

The Memory Stick / 9
Myth of Who I Am / 10
Sanctuary / 11
The Starting-Place / 12
The Things We Keep / 13
Cambodia / 14
Calendar Days / 15
Summer Nocturne / 16
Little Mysteries / 17
A Winter's Tale / 18
Perdelkino / 19
Red Star, Black Gates / 20
The Russian Delicatessen / 22
Fathers and Sons / 23
Soul Kitchen / 25
Loss / 26
Later / 27
Millenium Ode / 28
When All the Birds Were Called Away / 29
1957 / 30
Chant d'Amour / 31
She Walks on Diamonds / 32
Honeymoon / 33
Arrears / 34
It Was Autumn But He Called It The Fall / 35
The Blackbirds of Wilkinstown / 36
Poetry / 37
Port Oriel / 38
Petrarch's Muse / 40
Poem to a Granddaughter / 41
For Sophia / 42

Lisbon / 43
A Caravaggio Day / 44
Sojourn / 45
Looking for Vallejo / 46
Disillusionment / 47
The Collins Coat / 48
Neutral Ireland / 49
Islandbridge / 50
War / 51
The Last Voices / 52
Seven Reece Mews / 53
A Song of Elsewhere / 54
Wings of Desire / 55
Lament at the End of a Century / 56
A Long Story / 57
Letters from Beckett / 58
Poet and Blackbird / 59
Homage to Nick Drake / 60
Dancing in the Attic / 61
Ship in the Night / 63
Dog Years / 64
How Goes the Night? / 65
Poems to the Brides / 66
A Ruin in the Midlands / 68
Cold War Summer / 69
On the Cavan Bus / 70
Bounty / 71
Poem Beginnng with a Line by James Wright / 72
Mountain / 73
New Languages / 74
Vagabond Muse / 75
A Midwest Postscript / 76

for Simon, Karl, Joana, Laura and Sophia

The Memory Stick

All that was expected did not happen.
What we were most certain of never occurred.
It's all there on the memory stick:
where we were and what we did.
One day we were school leavers,
out the gate and gone in a hurry.
Those were days we wore dark colours
but still believed in the Light of the World
at the end of a summer when we carried
those books we borrowed but never returned
and shut out the world's disturbing news
by listening to Radio Luxembourg.

We let April pass, it had served its purpose –
grabbed with both hands summer's clover.
When our wedding meal was over
we rushed away from the long high table
to the honeymoon shore of pebbles and sand.
We composed our anthems on floors of raw wood
and soon after that discovered a short-cut
home to our cul-de-sac,
the house where we lay our heads
and spoke the praises of two March children,
breastfed at first, then weaned on words
and storybook tales out of this world.

Myth of Who I Am

She has lived so long with the myth of who I am.
Through the month of May blossoms,
the time of year for shooting stars and winter sun.
Through dark October evenings in the theatre,
starstruck by Hedda Gabler and King Lear.
Addicted to the minor chords, the cadences
of sadder songs I was the river-man
who knew the river's origin, who seized the chance
to be a dreamer on the river's banks;
a dreamer in the gallery where I stood rapt
before the *chiaroscuro* of Rembrandt.
She has lived so long with the myth of who I am:
bearer of poet's cramp, one who never tanned
in the almost blissful heat of foreign countries.

Sanctuary

There was a house of welcomes once
where those who practised time-honoured customs
never asked *Who is my neighbour*,
never cast a stone that hurt.

There was always a fatted calf,
an atmosphere of sanctuary under the raftered roof
and when the time came to depart
the last words said were *Come back soon*.

The Starting-Place

for Fiach and Bríd

Some mornings I walk through haunts
that remind me of who I was – a child
of mid-century, born in song-time after a war.

The place names have charms the places never had –
the alleyways of hurt and pride,
the street that became last stop of the wandering Jew,

home stretch of the many who were faithless
and the faithful few. I see what's gone,
what remains – a motherhouse that's empty,

the closed space of the Convent of Mercy.
The backroom where daylight was scarce
and night much darker than anywhere else.

From door to door I wonder who lives here now,
who sits at the table not touching breakfast,
not uttering what should be said.

In the locked-up church the bread
of life is going stale, the liturgies
are only words, dead on a page that's never turned.

The Things We Keep

for Angela O'Kelly

The things we keep are not the things we need:
the red flag and porcelain horse.
A calendar out of date since John Lennon was shot.
Those heaps that grow in the attic
and the garden shed: schoolbooks
of the old curriculum,
the winner's cup we refuse to relinquish,
a broken statue in salvaged shards;
black vinyl discs – each one with a groove
where the gramophone needle got stuck or skipped.
A carpenter's box with carpenter's tools,
a stack of cards from anniversaries
that added one more year to a love affair,
a marriage, a lost cause.
Soft toys reported missing long ago.
The Kodak camera bought with summer money –
a roll of film locked behind its shutter
holding secrets we'll never know.

The things we keep are not the things we need:
a map of London torn at the crease,
a postcard announcing that *This is the Life*
from someone on leave in the Eternal City.
Armfuls of news gone stale,
junk mail in praise of the local takeaway,
an old diary of pleasurable days,
a catechism with notes in the margins
on the doctrine of grace.
Ticket stubs from opening nights,
a holiday brochure for a land of blue skies
in the south, and keys with no purpose
since a childhood house was left to the dust.

Cambodia

for Simon

Our second son, the wanderer
has sent a postcard home that shows
the smiling people of Cambodia,
a Buddhist temple, a garden of magnolia.

On travels with his Mappa Mundi
he has stepped into this distant place
as far away as June's long days
are far from January. But he keeps in touch,

emails, texts – our second son, our Gulliver
who sends us words to describe his trek
through the killing fields on a tourist bus.
He calls it *another world*.

You'd never think there was a war on once,
he says – bombs and bullets, rockets, guns,
the house of love burning,
burning under the Asian sun.

Calendar Days

First signs of spring: the buds on the branches
appear without fuss, the forest turns greener
and offers us the scent of pine to breathe in.
May, June, July then August catching fire
before the cold blast of September
and the change of tempo when an ill-wind blows,
thrashing the rosebush out of shape.
We listen to the noise it makes agitating
the attic timbers. In the distance,
the helicopter with searchlights on,
trucks with their pin-ups and amulets of St Christopher.

The orchards empty, rose gardens strewn
with rose-confetti. We stay indoors,
doing humdrum things: flicking through the pages
of *Newsweek*, down-loading information
or in the chat-room making promises to strangers.

Our fathers and mothers established the customs
that we in our turn pass on to others –
in the murk of November
to burn a candle on All Souls Night.
On Christmas Eve keep doors unlatched,
place a light in the window, a light in the hall
to welcome the one returning
with branches of the holly,
who ends the year recalling it, the calendar days
that started with the killing frost, the January storms.

Summer Nocturne

for Maureen and Fergus

With hoof and claw animals are born tonight
and in the here-and-there of the countryside
there are glimpses of electric light.

Like ragged soldiers in retreat we are on the road,
back to where we came from, wheeling over hayseed,
corn-dust, carrion, proceeding with caution

through the only street in a darkened village.
Here and there in random places we find last vestiges
of a filling station or a parish hall

that used to be the destination of travelling-players.
A few starlings out late whisk the air
with their flying formation.

Waving goodbye to Maudlin Street, to that garden
planted with Blood of the Boyne apple trees
we slip into the flow of motorway traffic,

a journey flanked by sites of battle,
hay-bales standing in their short-lived shadows,
monuments to the summer that fattened them.

Little Mysteries

for Philip King

After a few false starts, the harmonica player
picks up a bluesy melody or slow air,
a cracked tune or one that was lost
and found, borrowed and returned
but never a burden to the one who carries it.
Maybe *Bless the Weather* or *Sweet Little Mystery*
or something more traditional
from a place that never runs out of rhythms
in the hills of Clare or Mississippi.

And blessed are the song-makers –
first the forgotten ones who sing no more
and now the troubadours of a new century chorus.
Theirs are the melodies that wander the earth,
from festival to festival
in those gardens where thousands pitch their tents

or that bit of a tune left in the air
when bow and fiddle are laid to rest
and the singer sits down,
his mouth dried up
like the red rose of blood on Connolly's shirt.

A Winter's Tale

A wedding ring falls from a bony finger,
a good-luck coin through a hole in a pocket.
The poets compose their odes to winter,
love sonnets to a river that needs to be cleaned.
The east wind blows like a wind at war
then moves north and that's a relief.
A crow in a field looks like a spot of ink,
the man who has a family, a home, a job,
a day in each week to honour his God
is robbed of these things in the middle of the night
or as daybreak sneaks from behind the clouds,
goes from house to house: those with their blinds
still down and the kitchen a mess
of unwashed delft, last night's dregs.

Perdelkino

His rows of books we are not let touch
and his portrait shows a sad expression
like the one that kept me looking
at the Mother of Sorrows in Kazan Church.

All is in order, the sleepy death mask –
a plaster cast without a scratch;
and furniture that's old-style
and still retains the aura of its former time.

His cap and coat still hang here,
as if he might come back someday –
the genius of the house to his hideaway
to pace the floors to Scribian's music,

Shakespeare's metres, vocables
taken by the roots into a second language.
In pride of place are the poet's daybed
and escritoire. At Peredelkino

he became a man with snow in his hair,
a scribe at scribe-work, serene in old age –
who heard the grass growing and the train
that kept going until the end of the story.

Moscow, June 2011

Red Star, Black Gates

In Moscow 1

Like an old scarecrow
that no longer scares the crows
Lenin on his plinth watches those
who pass – his gaze is fixed
on people who have not smiled
since Glasnost.
From a window near the sky
I survey a city so vast
it confounds the eye
and the heart. The boulevard
is a version of infinity,
a tapestry of citizens
on melancholy business.
They are spiritless
in the way they walk
and carry their nostalgia
for the red star on the shoulder
of the Cold War soldier.

In Moscow 2

By the Kremlin wall I sit and watch
a scene from Bulgakov. In my *Rough Guide*
there are names to conjure with:
the banished poets, the muses of lament
including one who wanted
the *city of wonder* taken out of her hands.
A trumpeter blows a Dixie melody –
more New Orleans than Moscow Central.
His halcyon tempo is from the days before I read
Anna Chrysostom of all the Russias or learned
about these black gates where Anna stood
in her dire moments of *everything plundered,
betrayed, sold, everything gnawed to the bone.*

The Russian Delicatessen

When the Russian delicatessen opened
opposite the Chinese takeaway,
I thought of my father and what he might say
to see this strange cuisine displayed
on one of his Dublin streets,
his hunting ground for life's necessities.
A street of apples and oranges,
where books were second-hand.
The quarter mile he walked like an earl
upon his land, up and down, from end to end,
an old habit he kept even when
he became a man of little appetite,
fooled by tricks of memory
and his luck ran out in the Saturday Derby.
A street where he stood on corners
to watch the passing of an age,
stood still to catch his breath at twelve
and six o'clock when the new electric bells
broke into song, an annunciation that made him pause,
straighten his shoulders and then walk on.

Fathers and Sons

1

Old father, only once I heard you whistle
a merry ditty, but I never caught the drift of it
on our Sunday morning stroll
through your favourite district along the river,
between cathedral spires, corner-shops,
as far the bridge you never crossed.

Horseplay and high jinks were not your style
old father, only once I heard you humming
a melody with snappy rhythms.
You were making tea and sweetening it,
old father, cog-in-the-wheel
until they replaced you with the new machine,
when the porter barrels changed from wood to steel –
only once I heard you curse,
it was under your breath in the oxygen tent,
when you heard the result of your five bob bet.

2

O children remember the summer
no rain fell, when we drove
through the Burren, up on the high roads
where there's no turning back
and after that childhood vanished in a puff:
Snow White and *Red Riding Hood*,
poisoned by the witch, eaten by the wolf.

From first breath to when you stood
like Prospero learning his magic
I hope my example was good,
that I passed on what you understand
of love and shielded you well from harm,
night terrors, the unwelcome guest,
gave you soft landings when you fell
so that you rose again ready to fly
like Superman into the yonder.

Soul Kitchen

She's here, install'd amid the kitchen ware.
— Walt Whitman

The washday bundle blows in the breeze, a row
of empty sleeves, the laundry sheet twisted like a shroud.
In the soul kitchen that tapping on the window
is a branch the pruning sheers missed.
Continuous tap-tapping that makes it sound as if
each time one story ends another begins.
I find you among your old recipes, calculating weights
and measures, in your cupped hand there are cherries –
a ripe bouquet of them. I watch as you sprinkle cinnamon,
break eggs, pour milk – all part of your repertoire of tricks.
It is the hour when the DJ talks to the listeners,
those who call to answer the quiz, send a greeting,
request a song with a melody as sweet as the melodies
of Keats who said the unheard ones were sweeter.

Loss

After the waves roll back
it's a longer walk down to the sea
where we hear the souls-in-torment shrieks
of white gulls in their parody of wild hysteria.

After the leaves have fallen,
on the day we look to find them gone
we see again the trees we call bare bones of winter –
a rigging of branches holding ragged nests
that all through summer were torn and mended.

After long negotiation there is failure to agree.
Flawless argument cannot save
the things we cherish: Tara's hill,
the holy well, the village in the glen
where they mourn the loss of the oral tradition.

Later

It is always later than you think,
late in the day, late in history –
too late to keep a diary of carnal pleasures
or be the chronicler of what must be
forgotten and forgiven.

No longer young-as-ever
you are like Narcissus who sees his face and weeps
because of the cracks and creases in it,
the lines of age, the rheumy eyes,
the purple veins no longer hidden.

It is always later than you think.
So late it's late into the season when the years
of the tree are cut down to be
paper for words not written yet,
a cradle or a marriage bed.

Millenium Ode

On the night the old century turned its back on us,
we filled the coal bucket and found a bundle
of sticks for the hearth that was cold all year.
We had our own music to raise the spirits,
our potent elixirs. The evening was one of silent
valedictions, of counting down to the seconds
before time began again. In the pause
between the passing and coming of days,
the millennial midnight came and went
with its bells and klaxons not to be tamed,
its revellers living a new jazz age.
While you kept to the warm side of the windowpane,
I slipped outside into the harsh night air
where like the actor who forgets his lines
I listened for the whisper from the wings, the prompt,
the hint, that bit of the script that gets us to the next scene.

When All the Birds Were Called Away

When the back door opened in a sudden gust
the noise of the birds hit a lull
as though all the birds were called away –
it was like the silence I heard once
in a great cathedral, a foreign church;
in the museum after Sunday lunch
when we were young in the age of boredom.

When all the birds were called away
it was like pause at the start of every song that's sung,
that moment in the jazz club
before they bang the cymbals and beat the drums
or like the hush in the stonebreaker's yard
where once historical drama was played
by poets, pedagogues, fanatical hearts.

1957

It was a time before I could tell
the hound of heaven from the hound of hell.
The coal-smoke clouds of 1957 were in the air.
Baking apples bought for Sunday
were carried home as if they were
the sorrows of the world.

That year technicolour was in vogue
and *Scarlet Ribbons* on the radio
was sung by Belafonte.
For a week I was kept upstairs in bed
with a rash that itched under my skin –
a rash like rings of fire.

Downstairs, an uncle on a long sabbatical
from the war was a soldier soldiering on –
one who knew what lies in store.
With a show of hands he played the spoons
and with his shoes tapped a tune
on the kitchen floor.

Chant d'Amour

You lay with me in a high room in Manhattan
and in a draught-riddled caravan.
You lay with me and made me laugh
by the riverside in Glengarriff,
on grass that stained your summer dress
and among the daisies that you chained
to hide the love bites on your neck.

I lay with you waiting for thunder to clear,
lightning to cease or watching sunrise
give the kiss of life to our window facing east.
You lay with me naked and lay with me wrapped
in blankets, quilts and soft eiderdown.
In heat wave and Atlantic storm,
with sand in our hair, or barleycorn
you lay with me on the shore beside a shrinking sea,
in a hayfield under the acorn tree.

She Walks on Diamonds

Snow that fell all afternoon
has left bus-stops desolate, avenues resplendent,
snow-roofs white as hospital beds.

Like the stain that spreads
when wine's knocked over by a sloppy guest
the colour comes back into her cheeks –

my beloved who with calm slow-motion steps
crosses the bridge that looks no different
from the swan's white breast –

the sparkle and glitter of it make her think
she walks on diamonds and not the snow-crust
on a path out to the suburbs.

At both ends of the street,
on both sides of the river, her steps leave tracks
like the ones in the wake of Breughel's hunters.

Honeymoon

Not the coast of Galicia, but the shores of Achill
in June, in honeymoon weather:
between sunshine and sunshowers
and the thunder you said was only the small gods
running across the island mountain.

From the heather beds of early summer
we dashed to the water, cold sand under heel –
you in that lemony garment of wool,
I in psychedelic shirt, not knowing which of us
was the lover and which the beloved.

Arrears

When it comes to love I am in arrears,
so much has been given
but not returned that I must seek forgiveness
for my disappearing act to that room
where I waited for the other muse,
forgiveness too for unspoken words,
long silences through the evenings
of our wedded lives: my inwardness, my absences
even when *I was there* at the kitchen table,
in the fireside chair – not *down-to-earth*
but gone from it in a deeper rapture
than the meditation-trance of a stoic-mystic.

It Was Autumn But He Called It *The Fall*

It was autumn but he called it *The Fall*.
The American uncle, home with his dollars
to the land of shillings and pence;
home with a twang in his voice
that made him sound like Eastwood in *Rawhide*.

He had come back after years,
his sojourn lasted weeks;
memories were the treasury he carried –
of the emigrant ship, the shore-to-shore Atlantic;
his first sight of an horizon

that was a latticework of fire escapes,
of buildings configured to hide the sky.
Home at last, he went looking for turf stacks
long turned to smoke and ash,
failed to recognise the woman who was a child

when he departed with his only inheritance,
the Brigid's Cross placed in his hands,
the one-way ticket to different pastures –
New York in its jazz age,
where a shy Hibernian boy hadn't the courage to dance.

The Blackbirds of Wilkinstown

> *It is spring now and it must be lovely down in*
> *Wilkinstown. Are the birds singing yet? When you*
> *hear a blackbird think of me.*
>   — Francis Ledwidge

There's a village where nothing has changed for years,
sweet pastures through which the railway track
is a memento kept as part of the scenery;
the bog where bog work was a tug-of-war,
where Ledwidge's blackbird flaunted her song.
The gatekeeper's cottage is gone, no need now
for the gatekeeper's morning and evening vigil.
The trees are like trees in a Russian novel –
tall and gaunt, some ready to fall
in the next winter storm. The righteous
have their inner sanctum: the country chapel
where they pray for the bride at the altar,
the soul in the box. No spectacle ever intrudes
except when the blackbirds arrive.
Through the sweet pastures, meeting ground
of the harriers, it's a short walk
from schoolhouse to cemetery where husbands
and wives are resting in peace
and stone walls keep a little of the sun's day-warmth
for night that comes darkening the harvested fields.

Poetry

That year was black with falls of soot
and clay dragged in from the cabbage patch.
Stray cats came and took their chance
until their bites drew blood and then
they disappeared in a drowning ceremony.
Rain poured through the thatch.

The dog with three legs went hopping mad,
barked at everyone who passed,
neighbours, strangers, the country doctor
who on the first of every month *looked in*
on the woman from the eighteen hundreds –
Grandmother who lived only

for the Mysteries of the Rosary
and told me once not to look for poetry
in the stars but out in the mucky yard
in the murmuring of the sally branches,
among the nettles and in the henhouse
and on the dungheap her chickens scratched.

Port Oriel

1.

There is more than one season
in the weather that comes
in on the grievous deep water
where once I saw an exodus
of boats in all colours leaving the harbour
in a retinue like father, mother and son.

Then at evening down at the pier:
The Rose of Sharon and *Rose of Dundalk*,
St Malachy berthed between them,
and the pier fishermen casting for strays
and holding their lines
as if they were pulling threads from the waves.

The sea damp could not be erased
from the trawl-nets knotted by storms
or the beds in the hostel buffeted by gales
so hard that sometimes it seemed like it could
slip anchor and sail from up
on the high road looking down on Port Oriel.

2. (Maggie)

In those last years of fading vision
she lived by the sea, hitched to a chair
in front of a vista of inlet and promontory
and off in the distance, the long peninsula –
Cooley and Carlingford,
the Celtic mountain or its misty similitude,
boats leaving the harbour, no sooner seen
than disappearing from her known world.

When she put away her book of folded corners
to look yonder, her eyes, half-blind,
were held in thrall by the pitch and toss
of the quicksilver tides come and gone
like the errand boy who climbed the hill
to her open door where the wind blew in
with a bang that even her deaf ear heard.

Petrarch's Muse

for Joana and Karl

From blazing moon to waning moon
the night passed there and then
at your Portuguese wedding.
Out in the garden the dark hours
were unravelling, the olive trees rained on
by rain that was filling the October rivers.

It was a long night of old hits and Fado tunes
not in translation but still conveying
the bitter-sweetness of every word,
saudade I had not heard since "Carrickfergus".

I went outside for a change of air,
a tree-shadow to hide in,
to gaze at the stars in their open-air theatre,
not one of them out of place,
the Plough or Orion or the distant nebula
in its excelsior haze.

I had on my mind that poem from Yeats –
his Delphic Oracle, the *choir of love* –
not knowing then the name of Petrarch's Muse
or that in time her name would sparkle on my tongue.

Poem to a Granddaughter

for Laura

On the drive from the airport
the road was your lullaby.
We took the straight route, left the detours
for another time.
Tucked in and safe in your backseat nest,
your eyes were closed, you slept
so did not see the garlands of light
the streets were wearing, or the way
the river makes the city two separate places,
parishes showing their age,
traces of the bygone barely remaining;
or the stately edifice where ash once flew
from the burning ledgers of the nation;
the library where I tiptoed among the books
with timeworn covers –
some not read for years, some not read at all,
forgotten like a flipside song
but waiting for someone like me
to begin at the prologue.
You were passing through
but I am held by the roots to this ground I walk on,
these places I know by name:
all that you saw when you opened your eyes
and looked around
at an old town best seen in the early light of day.

Christmas 2011

For Sophia

One day in the world and you became
a new face on my screen,
a new name to say and say again.

Some day you'll learn its Greek meaning
and be the voice that tells us
to cherish all we have.

We wait for years for days like these
when even the weedy flower is good to look at,
and the worm in the grass

and the ruin that was the palace of kings
and the dead leaves burgeoning in heaps
left by the late September winds.

In time you'll find your own enchanted way
like the first voyagers,
Vasco de Gama, Brendan the Navigator.

But before the journey you'll have to wait,
be still, observe; take nursery steps,
discover your sixth sense.

October 2014

Lisbon

> *Day after day I sweated up*
> *the seven hills of Lisbon*
> — Pearse Hutchinson

From a traveller's window
I gaze at the seven hills that left us footsore
after our journey to the poet's house –
an arduous walk until we reached the door
upon which we knocked four times,
once for each of the poet's lives.
Tramcars crawl the buckled streets
with passengers who want to view the panorama
of passing ships in Lisbon harbour,
the passageways of the Alfama.
On the Avenue of Liberation
there's a room for every guest
and on every floor corridor music
that repeats itself like Ravel's Bolero.
After breakfast they all disperse
through the Triumphal Arch, down to the bank
of the Tagus, running the gauntlet of restaurant tables.
In musty churches, where a few candles flicker,
there is shelter from the sun
that pours its glitter on the pleasure villas
and coast road where Odysseus stepped ashore
thirsty for the tears of Portugal.

A Caravaggio Day

for Paul, in Rome

Pluto, Neptune, Jupiter –
and the boytown boys with smiles
of ambiguity – he painted them
for a Prince of the Curia.
This man who took del Monte's coins,
who painted the cardsharp with a run of jacks,
Bacchus and the Baptist
and the tall Madonna with babe-in-arms
an infant Christ who looked
like any neighbour's child.

This man was dangerous,
a shooting star between shade and light,
a swaggerer down the long,
straight Corso, sword on hip;
a fugitive through the back-street labyrinth,
looking for a safe roof,
on the run from his accusers.

Chasing the ship that abandoned him,
the sea became his final provocation,
this man who painted Paul of Tarsus
fallen from his horse –
Soldier Saul soon to learn
that every station is a Station of the Cross.

Sojourn

> *I was a free man in Paris,*
> *I felt unfettered and alive*
> — Joni Mitchell

Little by little I learned the map
and followed its routes, using it to the full
until the map was part of me
and written into the chronicle of my sojourn.
Dull days and days of radiance,
of walking on and on between the traces
of regency and revolution, reading inscriptions
and reading the stains on Danton's orations
in second-hand bookstores by the Seine.

Little by little I learned the map:
the holy places and secular temples,
the long road down from Belleville
to visit Proust and Wilde and Eluard.
Little by little I learned the map:
the riverside kiosks with their battered
editions of Jean Paul Sartre,
the bridge of "love locks" and where to avoid
the marching mob and riot squads
by taking backstreets not in the guide
because they are ways that never catch the sun.

Looking for Vallejo

in Montparnasse

Among the monuments they still mourn for Serge
and do a sentimental dance,
those women who keep the flowers fresh
and drop the ash from cigarettes
upon the grave that is now his mask.
But you Vallejo, you too were there on the map
of the dead but I could not find you
in your corner of Division Twelve.

Twice I came – on Sunday morning,
then in Thursday rain; through the iron gates
into your season of repose where you, cut loose
from all maladies and discord,
the martyrdoms of blood and brute force,
were there on the map of the dead –
there since Good Friday broke your lease on life,
your last sunrise, last chance to throw the eternal dice,
dip your pen in ink and write the changes
to that poem of conjuration:

Caesar Vallejo is dead, they nailed him down.

Disillusionment

We have seen it at the head of the march,
seen it dance, seen it dangle:
the flag the south wind catches.
It is part of the pomp, pageant fodder –
the billowy tricolour hoisted in honour
of the seven back from purdah:
Plunkett, Clarke, McDermott, Ceannt,
Connolly, Pearse, McDonagh.

It is the flag they carry when the State
pays homage with drums, salutes and rhetoric
less honest than the men it praises –
Tone and *Davis* and whoever else
is still remembered when they lay a wreath
for all the dead beside the monument,
under the epitaph for those
who if they reappeared to form a circle
would see a time of yearning,
the consequence of sorry days:
our Aegean stables
but no Hercules to clean them.

The Collins Coat

Look at it now, the greatcoat worn by him
in the cloud weather of the south, in the assassin's
gimlet view. Imagine this – the sway

and swish of it, harp-buttons aglitter,
as he made his way through the hiss of enmities,
clenched fists, the whispered and shouted

oaths of allegiance. Hard shoulders, long sleeves
fit for the arms he raised at the monster meetings
or when he was ready to sign on the dotted line:

death warrants, treaties. Thick wool of military green
worn into shape by a nation-builder's
girth – the cut of it a clear outline

filling its own glass shrine. And so it became
his shroud – this mantle, garment, sagging weight
of collar and hem, with pockets that once held

the wiles of war and peace, the gun in politics.

Neutral Ireland

When the lights were out in Europe
in neutral Ireland we had
the light of kitchen fires, cottage lamps
and the light when lightning strikes
a holy place. In neutral Ireland
we had nothing to loose,
folk-cures were in demand,
stone walls of Connemara
leaned a little to one side,
men in the family joined
the armies of church and state.
In the towns where the same man
buried the dead and sold their land
there were nights of dancing,
afternoons of cheers and chants
and county teams trampling
the playing field grass
and on the shore there was always
someone to wave farewell,
someone whose voice never failed
to shout *Godspeed the emigrant.*

Islandbridge

The river heron and the young canoeist rowing
past the picnic tables and war memorial
go by with the speed of those in a hurry.

In less than a moment they are gone
just like the men who wore grey beards when I was young,
stoic and silent when their wars were over,

their medals lost among the knick-knacks
of cottages on Long Lane
or sold to the moneylender who knew they'd never

be reclaimed or worn on Poppy Day.
Theirs was a new nation without a guiding star,
those men who lived on to know their day was gone

and in the dreams of afternoon sleep
feel again the itch of a Tommy's uniform
and the blast that threw them into the arms of mercy

when the big guns opened fire.

War

in memory of Jack Smyth, Pimlico, Dublin

A child asked *What is war*
and the old soldier remembered
it is the place where men forget where they are,

it is night in the Dardanelles,
the generals at supper, the Tommy on watch:
a vigil-keeper holding his breath

in rain that comes one step after another.
It is advance and retreat on the roads of France,
courage to be with the dead,

the battle with no intermissions,
a dry-run drenched in the blood of sons,
the strong arm needed to carry the wounded

to the surgeon's table
that stands adjacent to the graveyard worms.
It is the curse on the map of Europe,

a country no one has heard of,
the big mistake of the fool
who thinks it can bring back peace.

It is what William Orpen saw,
sometimes through a soft blur.

The Last Voices

> *And life slips by like a field mouse*
> *Not shaking the grass.*
>   — *Ezra Pound*

In the morning we carried the warm bread.
In the evening we sat on the cooling steps.
In the corner tavern the TV set
was a blurry image of the stately president
walking with his walking stick,
silver-tongued in two languages.

We were the last voices,
out late, in the dusky heat of summertime,
pretending not to hear our names
when they were called
but hearing only the volley shots
of the handball against the walls
of Margaret's Avenue and the timber yard
where all day long the electric saws
went through their repertoire
of chimes and chants and skittish staccato.

As the day declined, it was suppertime
in our Eldorado,
but we were savouring the brief pause
before the light withdraws,
before the final call to end our games and talk –
to come indoors to where the clocks
were ticking and old men sang their rebel songs.

  for Paul Doyle on his 60th birthday

Seven Reece Mews

Up rope-railed steps he climbed to his true life,
his win-some, lose-some time in the studio
under rafters and roof-window –
amid the mess of things he couldn't relinquish:
hardened colours, painter's brushes,
film-stills from *Hiroshima, Mon Amour*.

Standing room only between the pictures cast aside,
renounced, rejected, half-destroyed
by scissor-cut and slash of Stanley knife.
Not for the connoisseur of beauty his prince
of benedictions howling the Holy Name,
his whittled image of the Sphinx,
or his portrait sitters like convalescents learning
to live with body torments, diseases of the flesh.

A Song of Elsewhere

How close they are in the age of Google map:
the roads to Athens and Alexanderplatz,
the ancient cathedrals of Italy and France;

the vineyards and fig orchards
along the Camino track, Prague's moody
perspective of statues and bridges,
Ljubljana where the exit signs are riddles.

Venice, its artistry and splendour
and numerous ways to arrive at the same
moment twice; its light fluorescing
the Doge's Palace and gilding the delta.

How close they are in the age of Google map:
the places where we land
and disembark: the cities of nomads,
Babylonian crowds –

on inland hills, at the edge of sea-mist,
where district lines and exhausted rivers
divide the destinations of the poor and rich.

Wings of Desire

In November when night appears
at four o'clock and a chilling mist caps the domes
of church and synagogue, they were selling as souvenirs
fragments from the wall of death – the wall that divided
west from east. Over the traces of Kristallnacht,
they have built the fashionable streets, laid down the tracks
that run each way. At the Brandenburg Gate,
in the Starbucks café, in a metropolis
where every photograph we took turned out grey,
we sat and watched the Monument to Victory,
her swarthy horses giddying. Then we went looking
for all the places the angel visited in *Wings of Desire*.

Lament at the End of a Century

Those who saw it say they never saw it coming –
poets in uniform on a battlefield of mud,
the evening star above them.
The workhorse giving way to new machinery,
colonies abandoned, the first moon-landing
by astronauts whose shadows fell on cosmic dust,
whose walk, much like a child's on a trampoline,
is now ghost-footage.

Those who saw it say they never saw it coming –
the newsflash interrupting
normal transmission when the princess in the tunnel
had no prince to save her.
Then the send-off she received
from the bells of the city, all the showbiz tears,
the pigeons of Piccadilly summoned into the air.

Those who saw it say they never saw it coming –
in the age of fibre optics,
the Dark Ages returning and messages delivered
in the instant it takes to travel the world.

A Long Story

It's a long story between Gregorian chant
and the beats of electronica:
there's the featherweight sonata
on which we drift away,
the fecundity of Mozart,
adagios of Mahler, the back-to-back
lives of Schubert and Brahms
with their symphonies of strings and brass.

It's a long story
between Vienna's fairytale waltz
and *The Fairytale of New York*,
between Bach and modern jazz:
Bach, the keeper of flocks,
of places where sheep could safely graze.
The Art of Fugue, its coming of age
passed on but the Art of Fugue became
music for the hour of rapture,
the sound of wheels on fire.

Letters from Beckett

> *I need a thousand years of silence.*
> – Letter to Jerome Lindon

From Rue de Favorites and Ussy-sur-Marne
and somewhere between languages
your epistles arrived, some chatty,
some terse – sealed with a kiss
from your Giacometti lips.

Letters ripe with *Mon chére* and *chérie,*
language stripped to artful sentences,
a poet's metaphors, with no time
for the trivia of boulevard banter
or terms of endearment that wither

as soon as they're written.
Through Foxrock, Enniskillen, Saint-Lo,
the monotony of Gertrude Street
you lived the life of pimpernel and scribe,
a brother to the unnameable.

Poet and Blackbird

for Sheila Pratschke, on the occasion of Seamus Heaney's reading at the Centre Culturel Irlandais, Paris, June 2013

When the poet handed that blackbird glad notes to sing,
it was not a voice from the Blaskets I heard
but the evening chanteuse of the Latin Quarter,
who then lay down exhausted on her high altar
and let the poet get on with his own loved music.

In light that burnished every stone
the sky was clear, the bell was hushed
in praise of the gifts of the tongue.
The stones, though small and easily shuffled,
were stepping stones to lyric utterance.

We were *souls in a flock at twilight*,
our compound a Belle Isle for one night,
finding place-names from home in a foreign corner,
reminders of our *Irlandais*, little whispers

from Elphin and Ossory, Derry and Dublin –
all in praise of the gifts of the tongue:
the poet singing the pages of Guillevic,
the blackbird home on the range, silently watchful.

Homage to Nick Drake

for Sasha Dugdale

Like Mary Jane, his tresses were long.
He was a new Caedmon,
bard of a halcyon summer –
of the downs and the shires,
sweet hedgerows and apple orchards,
the Lady Chapels and healing waters.

With brooding heart and eyes downcast
he wandered the forests
where all must lose their way
and sang in a low croon,
with cellos around him, under leaf-shade
that had sheltered Hardy and Browning.

He was a new Caedmon,
last keeper of the Romantic Sublime,
of an England of the lark ascending,
the plough horse walking the furrow –
Ely, Canterbury, Tanworth-in-Arden;
cathedral choirs singing *Day is Done*.

Dancing in the Attic

in memory of Ann Brien

1

It might have been called *The Kingdom of Heaven* –
that discotheque in attic space
that was the heartbeat of the night.
A crowd of strangers dancing with strangers –
the atmosphere so dimly lit it was hard to find a face
among the girls with airs and graces,
and the *Johnny-Come-Latelys*,
hands in their pockets, backs to the wall.

Same as always, in faded jeans
and check shirts hanging loose,
we wandered in, hearkening to Martha Reeves,
sometimes the beat of *Born on the Bayou*.
On the stroke of twelve the music stops
the DJ pulls the plug, house-lights come on –
so metallic and bright they could be searchlights
looking for escapees along the Berlin Wall.

2

In a Sixties dive, a Sixties turntable
was spinning the vinyl: the poet from Montreal
saluted the Sisters of Mercy, the troubadour
from Minnesota was pitying the Poor Emigrant.

To pass the boredom, girls were dancing wildly,
humming the chorus of a song from Merseyside.

It was a place to go on Saturday night to slake a thirst,
tie a love-knot or to find a consolation.

A Sixties dive, a house divided into rooms of homely
exile: dull surroundings of plywood and Formica
but beckoning with its blandishments –
German wine, home brew, apple cider.

Ship in the Night

Falling from the ether, coming in on the tides
the Age of Aquarius arrived
with its pole star to the west
and California weather,
a time for the love-in, the street fight,
for the sorceries of the blues guitarist,
gentler strings for the broken-hearted.
The needle in the groove
scratched the tunes of a new troubadour.

In grandmother's halfway house
I was the boy who listened for hours
to radio broadcasts from a ship in the night.
A ship far from shore, with nowhere to go –
that hoisted a flag of convenience
above its cargo of songs in the morning,
songs in the moonlight,
the chanson of the chanteuse
who kindled desire in every man she knew –
my night-companion who sang me to sleep
with her blues that she blew
in on the tides and out of the ether.

Dog Years

In the middle of the night her bark was one
that seemed to reach the point of ecstasy.
Fireworks and wind-chimes frightened her,
our little dog who lived through the changes,
devoured chocolate and Pavlova,
loved to lick the honey jar.
Because dog years add up to so many
when she was old we thought she was young –
our terrier with grinding jaw, toothed grin,
who preferred to amble, never run,
whose silent five-word prayer was *Give the dog a bone.*
She slept with one eye open
to see the small, thin birds of spring
and with masterstrokes of nose and tongue
sought attention, and pawed me when
I was in the middle of a Berryman Dream Song
of *homage and soft remorse*
or one of Brodsky's sonnets to Mary Queen of Scots.

How Goes the Night?

It goes like this: sleepless since
the thumping beat of a car-stereo
broke the peace and headlight beams
crossed the ceiling, going east
then disappearing in the corner
where the spider lives.

Idle thoughts, erotic longings;
a list of tasks to think about –
but no lush soundtrack to sweeten the dark
in the theatre of the mind
just the vigil of a digital clock
watching with the red eyes of a god.

Poems to the Brides

1. *for Sinéad and Martin*

Last night you were nobody's wife
with time to wander, time to stop
on every corner, at the hooded window
of the *maison de chocolat*.

But today in this reprieve from summer rain
you keep the rendezvous you arranged
in the House of the Lord
where a nineteenth century poet-priest
begged Christ to pull the thorn from his side.

Today is a day to kick your heels
to the warm-up tunes, but first you must pay heed
and listen to Old Testament advice on marriage,
on a good wife's virtues –
mistranslated from the Book of Sirach.

2. *for Belinda and Aengus*

The bride wore a dress lost for years
but found in time for late revisions
to the vintage lace that touched the ground
she walked with stealth like a high-wire artist
following the almost-invisible line.

And a bell rang out to summon the guests
into the tent of *plain hearts* and *country pleasures*.

Lights from a fairground shone through the trees.
Howls from the Ferris-wheel and the merry-go-round
were heard in the distance across the valley of streams.

A Ruin in the Midlands

> *But I woke in an old ruin that the winds howled through*
> – W B Yeats

Back in the age of candlelight and grandeur,
of banquets in the chieftain's mansion,
there was meat and drink
for the ladies and the lords
and tunes upon the harpsichord.

But all that is history, the candle-factory
ceased to prosper, ceased to exist.
In the ruins of the chieftain's mansion
there are trespassers in a state of bliss.
They are there for the dope and the pills.

There's a cider-party, a ghetto-blaster
blasting Lady Gaga; chicken bones
and burger wrappers littering what remains
of the halls of marble, the rooms without tapestries
where phantoms go about their useless tasks.

Cold War Summer

In the days when marvels were the first satellites
transmitting their signals,
the heart surgeon performing his miracles;
when the bright evenings seemed to grow on trees
in the public park, a schoolboy
with whole chapters to read, maps to study
preferred instead long walks that took him
on a reconnoitring mission, beginning on the street
where anxious pigeons pecked the gutters
then past the shabby vistas and eyesores of the city,
down the hill where City Hall stands,
under the arch and over the bridge
to see the crowds waiting for tickets
for *The Fall of the Roman Empire*.

At first his wanders were never far,
just to see a poster outside a downtown cinema,
the Corinthian or Astor, where the movie stars
were Continental, the movies *Nouvelle Vague*
but often in those days the censor's blade
had been at work and scenes were cut, lovers erased.
At first his wanders were solitary,
a getaway into the world of strangers, the library
where books were stamped with a date
for their return, a day in the future
that might never come in the chill of a Cold War summer.

On the Cavan Bus

These country roads meander a little
like Odysseus coming home
or tunes not written down, but improvised.
All along the way I feel the tug
of signpost names: *Kells, Oldcastle, Ballyjamesduff.*

On the Cavan bus, the way is long
but the scenery is a grassy idyll
as we get closer to Virginia.
The rain-beaten hills are drying in the sun
and rainclouds on the run have gone
with the travelling musicians who had to travel on
with banjo, fiddle, accordion.

Through hay-scented meadowland
these lanes meander a little, take detours
like the cortège going back to pause
at the house of the deceased –
these lanes that were leafy once until the trees
were butchered, the ditches stripped of lushness
by someone who thought this place should be
like someplace else.

Bounty

in memory of Caroline Walsh

Here's a memory, you with your head in the bounty
cupboard, rooting and digging
for the one book hidden by all the others.

And here's a memory in different colours,
your laugh that showered its sparks on us,
red lipstick on the rim of a coffee cup

or your straw bag stuffed with pages
of revisions to the countless ways of telling a story,
your fresh editions of the fiction-makers

of Mitteleuropa, the American south –
whatever came in the morning post:
the estimable book of lyrics and odes, a new account

of historic times. Here's a memory that's musical:
the sudden surprise of your singing voice
hitting the notes of a Neil Young tune,

after one of those high-speed conversations
when you'd ask about the Dublin Jews
of Clanbrassil Street or quote a line from *Tate's Avenue*.

Poem Beginnng with a Line by James Wright

in memory of Dennis O'Driscoll

I dream of his slow voice, flying
between the Book of Laws and the Book of Poetry.
His voice on the answer machine
telling me he is not home –
a voice so calm I want it beside me on the dark road
and on days our island is under clouds
that make us want to shout
O give us back the mornings of more light.

A voice born in the princedom of song;
easeful as Latin chant or the late-night nocturne –
I want it as my guide on a Tipperary mountainside
and on my walk in the city when I set out to find
lost memories in the place I come from
and where I learned in a distant age
that there are blemishes we carry from birth,
dark moods we wear like an everyday shroud.

Mountain

for Francis Harvey

Perhaps I never stopped to look
or all the days were days of hurry,
of running with news, running too fast.

Or did I see it once
and ever after take it for granted –
never gave it a second glance –

the passive mountain, far-off but in view –
clear and visible from my city window.
Its evening silhouette is the contour

of a forest, taller every year.
Sometimes it blocks the sun, in snow-time
it becomes a cold white altar.

All my life it has been there – that glimpse
of distant peaks, a vista I was given
between two corners of a street.

That same old street
where I took a thousand steps
and met my first enchantress.

New Languages

When I heard the new languages,
peculiar idioms on the street,
I heard Africa and Gdansk
in broken fragments
and knew the world was changing,
that Joyce's town of lover-boys
and their Jezebels had lost its voice,
gone under the tides and disappeared.

The new languages had sweet
and bitter words that I heard when I sat
beside the immigrant on the city bus,
the one who will play his part
in the comedies and tragedies
of my old neighbourhood,
whose children will someday ask:
Who was Peig and who was Stephen Dedalus?

The new languages were added to the soundtrack
of the General Post Office and Moore Street
markets. They travelled so far
it was as if they came from the galaxies,
not Vilnius nor a province on the map of China
or close to where a desert journey begins,
places whose story is rewritten many times
until no story exists.

Vagabond Muse

for Eugene O'Connell

There is no sage I want to follow
except perhaps the one whose tapping finger
tapped me on the shoulder long ago:

the vagabond muse whose mood-swings
I am used to, whose tunes come in from near
and far: a lulling chant, a marching rhythm.

Heartless, tender, sometimes so long missing
and out of reach, the vagabond muse
leaves me like the watcher keeping vigil,

guessing where to look, when to listen
for the riffs that come from earth and air,
the ghost poet who is and isn't there.

A Midwest Postscript

1. ON MICHIGAN AVENUE

In the Art Institute Hopper's *Nighthawks*
have a life of their own.
But out here this wind could work for a butcher,
the way its cuts through flesh and bone –
it's a heartbreaker, head-wrecker,
destroyer of the soul.

With its cold cold fingers.
what it does to the body is mean.
We bite and it bites back, it makes the wheel
of fate go round.

In this city of pilgrims
where the light has a watery taste
I'm a pilgrim searching for Willie Dixon,
listening for his *Hoochie Coochie Man*
but hear only the rattle of trains on the "L"
and a saxophone howling on Michigan Avenue.

2. BIG SKIES

No fences here where the only visitor
is the blizzard or twister,
where cornstalks wither and the long roads are clear.

The silos look forlorn, exposed –
but each one holds something that is noble,
a harvest of grain or harvest of stories.

The eagle, the buzzard, the wild turkey
are living the moment in their elemental world.
On the five-dollar map there are traces

of France in the nomenclature: St Croix,
St Cloud, La Salle but closer to legend
are Redwood Falls, Stillwater, Minnehaha.

It is not the quickest way through American history,
this train that trundles under big skies,
carrying us down banks of the Mississippi –

that river that runs like a slow fuse, north to south
that passes through places where they do not live
by bread alone, do not seek the consolations of the city.

3. TORNADO DAY

The sirens blow their warning just to say
that today is Tornado Day in Minnesota.

But that sky that's a shade
between blue and grey looks calm
not angry, not ready to be on the front page
in cinematic images or release a swirling dervish
to dance on the graves of old Indians.

Here where the land goes on forever
and a bootlegger took up squatter's rights
there are fifty ways to get to one place:
the bowling alley, the mall, the State archives;
the neighbourhoods that have changed
their fidelities once or twice.

Behind the slow school bus
we drive the length of Cherokee Boulevard.

In full solemnity the flag of the nation
is breasting the air on weathered front porches
where pumpkin heads remain from the last celebration
and Christmas bouquets are still nailed to doors
on the nineteenth of April.

    for Jean and Jim Rogers

4. A JUKEBOX IN MINNESOTA

A coin in a jukebox in Minnesota
was the price of a song
to placate the gods of St Paul,
of Duluth where a greenhorn
heard the lovesick and rueful Opry star
and the bluesman, light-fingered
on his travelling guitar.

Highland snows were beginning to thaw
when out of that wilderness of iron ore
the singing man with harmonica,
stepped into the arena, proclaimed a new order.

But it's no real life being the one
who has to stay *forever young*: a gypsy scholar
on speedway and ocean, and be as well
the shaman, messenger, joker
in tune with perpetual motion.
Father of Jacob, son of Abram, a Jack of Hearts
who like Lazarus received a second chance.

5. Twin Cities

An April thaw has whittled away the last snow-patch.
Crossing from city to city, my journey unlike the exodus
out of Egypt is not a panic dash
but an easy ride on chrome wheels,
under destination signs on Franklin Avenue.

From the river bend I catch sight of it and freeze –
the bridge that tells me all I need to know,
where Berryman's leap was a vengeance
on the world and its Court of Appeals.

That was years ago, in one of the twin cities:
not St Paul but Minneapolis where tonight after browsing
a bookstore for the folklore of the prairie
I forget my way and stop a cab
whose driver from Somalia puts his faith in the Satvav
but keeps a prayer-rug under his seat.

6 Meeting Robert Bly

He studies us, the way a sailor studies the horizon.
The poet with broad shoulders, a corn-picker's shadow;
who yesterday *saw a face that gave off light*,
who today sits with his back to the door,
his gaze directed at the apple of his eye.

He is back from going his own way,
days on the farm, nights at the desk of solitude;
through cropland where the thresher was abandoned,
or leaving his tracks in snow that blanked the field
of white roses. He is listening for a shift

in the earth's axis under the weight of the granaries
and knows where to find the stolen child
in the hiding places of the Lake Isle and Madison.
He is listening too for the mouse that scratches
the floor of his heavenly mansion.

7. HIGHWAY 61

Somewhere off the highway of mythologies
there is a town worth visiting for an afternoon interlude,
where someone with local knowledge
shows us the penal walls, then the graves of soldiers
in the civil war cemetery.

There were towns like this I saw once
in Hollywood westerns in the *Cinema De Luxe*.
That was when I lived in two worlds –
the one in the heart-thumping noise of the streets
and the one on the screen while the lights were out.

Somewhere off the highway of mythologies
there is a bar that offers Midwestern solitude,
a place for the wayfarer,
and the migrant worker in from the fields,

a place for the riverboat captain who has seen
the river bluffs play hide-and-seek in the offshore mist
and wondered were they really there
or half-imagined like buried treasure.

for Thomas Dillon Redshaw

8. Another American Twilight

Another American day,
mission bells and Jericho trumpets,
the car-wash doing its rumba,
a hot dance in the grey arctic temperature.
They say that here is a hard station
until spring and the thaw
and ice becoming water again
and that stretch in the evening
when the central star is clear to the eye.

Another American twilight,
a time to praise the modern neighbourhood
with hidden cameras,
the great lakes that have their mariners,
freight trains travelling
where there is no end to the track,
the bars with Irish names
serving the beers of America,
dew-in-a-bottle from a highland distillery.

9. Timbertown

The motels of the Midwest are like orphanages:
windows dressed in old lace, sheets the colour of ash.

They are the opposite of opulence,
the last resort for beds that sag,
broken furniture, the lullaby of a jazz trumpeter.

There's a place by the window where it's possible to see
a different world, the swoops of a bird of prey,
sunset and its domino effect.

There is no gold or jewels or gambler's fortune
locked in the safe – when you have to pay
it's cash they seek, not *American Express*.

The one-night residents: runaway, salesman, transient,
wake up tired, still needing rest; sick of the smell
of detergent coming through walls
of breeze-block and lumber hewn from the logs
that made Timbertown prosperous.

9. MISSISSIPPI

The local river carries its name from one end
to the other, from the lake in the north to the delta
in the south; passing through the land of God

the first stranger it meets is the devil
learning to swim, plunging in
but keeping away from the Christening pool.

Sometimes it turns to mud in the muddy creek
or breaks loose to seek the Governor's
Mansion on the way to Baton Rouge.

In its waters there are bones, there is blood.
There are towns that need it
and towns it washes away in a punishing flood.

Little has changed since the slave looked at it
and saw freedom; since an image of the river
was painted to hang in the county museum.

The local river knows the lonely despair of the loner
and the light of transfiguration, light that shows
the poverty of trees when they are out of season.

10. TRAIN RIDE THROUGH WISCONSIN

On the train-ride through Wisconsin I saw Wisconsin,
not the people with their unhappy faces
just the land but not the whole expanse of it –
farm tracts that made me think of the scene
in *Days of Heaven* when the locusts came,
an army of them looking ominous, sent by the deities
to cause havoc, teach a lesson –
then the scene in which colliding horses
were the horses of the apocalypse.
From the window of the train I saw Wisconsin:
the undressed beauty of its fields,
mile after mile of cosmic stillness
that seemed to grip the water towers and shacks
in which, I like to think, outlaws lived.

11. GLIMMERINGS

A Minnesota Dream Song

The first day in Minnesota is always the worst.
Your body-clock lives in two places at once,
you only want to sleep but outside it's vintage America,
the school bus waiting for latecomers,
the garbage collectors raising dust.
High-steppers practise their twirls
on the stadium grass.

The way the weather breathes into your ear
is like a snake's hiss.
The pilgrim settles into the bunkhouse –
a room paid for in advance.
He has come a long way
to where his mission is to find those *glimmerings* again –
among the tree-shapes, along the ridges
or down the track to a panoramic vista
that seems to whisper lines from Whitman:

Night on the prairies,
The supper is over, the fire on the ground burns low.

www.ingramcontent.com/pod-product-compliance
Lightning Source LLC
LaVergne TN
LVHW041344080426
835512LV00006B/607